WINNING MORE BUSINESSES

How Martech and Salestech Increase Results of Marketing and Sales

Stephan S. Sunn

Davidson Global & Co.

Copyright © 2024 Stephan Sunn

©Copyright 2024 -2026 Stephan Sun All Rights Reserved

Disclaimer:

This book may not be reproduced or transmitted in any form without the written permission of the authors. Every effort has been made to make this guide as complete and accurate as possible. Although the authors have prepared this guide with the greatest of care, and have made every effort to ensure its accuracy, we assume no responsibility or liability for errors, inaccuracies, or omissions. Before you begin, check with the appropriate authorities to ensure compliance with all laws and regulations. Every effort has been made to make this report as complete and accurate as possible. However, there may be mistakes in typography or content. Also, this report contains information on online marketing and technology only up to the publishing date. Therefore, this report should be used as a guide – not as the ultimate source of Internet marketing information. The purpose of this report is to educate. The authors do not warrant that the information contained in this report is fully complete and shall not be responsible for any errors or omissions. The authors shall have neither liability nor responsibility to any person or entity concerning any loss or damage caused or alleged to be caused directly or indirectly by this report, nor do we make any claims or promises of our ability to generate income by using any of this information.

Davidson Global Partners & Co. LLC, Davidson, NC 28036, USA ; All Inquiries of copyrights, and cooperation go to: Stephan.sunn@aya.yale.edu

CONTENTS

Copyright 3
Preface 3
Chapter 1: Digital Ocean of Economy 3
Chapter 2: Understanding Martech and Salestech 3
Chapter 3: Leveraging Martech for Marketing Success 3
Chapter 4: Empowering Sales with Salestech 3
Chapter 5: Integrating Martech and Salestech 3
Chapter 6: Navigating the Digital Ecosystem 3
Chapter 7: Challenges in Digital Transformation 3
Chapter 8: Global Expansion and Localization Strategies 3
Chapter 9: Future Trends in Martech and Salestech 3
Chapter 10: Success Cases for References 3
Acknowledgement 3
About The Author 3
Books By This Author 3
Title Page 1

PREFACE

The author of this book series and their partners possess over 20 years of experience in their respective fields. They are widely recognized and respected within their professional communities and international networks. Prior to the pandemic, this group would convene at least once a year at locations around the globe. We were grateful to be healthy when we met for the first time after that global catastrophe.

When we resumed meeting, the realization that life is fragile and fleeting prompted an idea about the merits of documenting our work, successes or failures, so our colleagues now and future could benefit from it. With the 2022 arrival of ChatGPT and other groundbreaking AI technologies, we concurred on the urgency to expedite this documentation before such innovations fundamentally transform our lives and society, akin to the impact of COVID-19.

This book series focuses on the business domains in which we have supported clients worldwide last two decades. While the structure may not adhere to academically logical or analytically procedural norms, each major section evidences its importance in increasing the probability of success, enhancing production efficiency, or improving return on investment. Each book culminates with a "Chapter of Lessons" that summarizes some of the frequently encountered pitfalls in our practices. For privacy and confidentiality, public examples illustrate these lessons.

Marketing leaders are reinventing their roles while simultaneously enabling their team members to explore new ways of working. The intersection of marketing, sales, and technology is increasingly critical but is often hindered by competing priorities, a lack of understanding, and even open hostility.

Many marketing leaders believe the next 18 months will see a greater change in the role of technology than we have seen in the past two decades. Effective integration of Martech and Salestech has the potential to create a competitive advantage at a time when many customer journeys have reached a level of maturity in some global markets while at the same time, overlapping to an uncomfortable degree.

CHAPTER 1: DIGITAL OCEAN OF ECONOMY

The Digital Ocean is the age of business we live in today where small or big corporations are trying to stay afloat in an overcrowded, market-saturated, and interconnected world. It is essential for businesses of all sizes to understand and implement the two dynamic tools or channels reshaping business exchanges or transactions profoundly: Martech and Salestech. With a click of a button, technological advancements allow businesses to target specific customers and allocate matching resources to the critical leads. These two tools are the reason that 200+ technology products checked into The Technology Garden today are able to guide executives or governmental authorities to make necessary adjustments to get the treasures without conflicts with rhinos.

Defining the Digital Landscape; Its Disruptive Impact on Businesses

The digital landscape is the business environment that companies have to navigate due to the rise and widespread use of the internet in previously non-internet-related companies. This means that even companies who don't explicitly function in the digital sphere such as a widget manufacturer must keep up online. If you want to know more about Internet Marketing visit us at www.ProfitBooks.com. Professors lecturing on business strategy might liken the digital landscape to Porter's 5 forces. Just as largely unrelated companies owe their success or their destruction to industry dynamics like the power of suppliers/buyers, barriers to entry, etc. so do companies owe their success or destruction to Amazon, Google, LinkedIn, Salesforce, and Microsoft due to the rise and widespread use of the internet. The digital arena includes, but is not limited to, channels that your prospects and customers read often.

Perhaps no other aspect of the digital landscape is more significant than the ability to connect with potential customers so precisely and quickly. In the age of wireless internet enabled by the latest AI, individual or corporate customers are more connected than ever before. They have more knowledge, more choices, more threats, and more influences at their fingertips than any other consumers in history. Customer power created by this unprecedented level of connectivity is changing the power relationships between customers and businesses. This customer-powered reality means that businesses have to work harder than ever to get the attention and keep the attention of customers across a growing number of digital touchpoints.

The digital revolution has also spawned new forms of competition and collaboration. Digital platforms have lowered the cost of entry for new entrants, enabling startups and small players to challenge established incumbents. The interconnected nature of the digital world has also led to a new kind of balance of power between companies that specialize in a certain space, with quite a few key technologies such as Apple's iPhone being a collection of hardware and software technologies from several firms - so among the companies and industries attending the executive programs, alliances and industry partnerships - often between onetime rivals - have been multiplying every week.

The Rise of Martech and Salestech

Today, companies are investing in Martech and Salestech solutions to help them navigate the complex digital landscape. Martech refers to the suite of technologies and tools designed to help marketers more effectively reach, engage, and convert customers in the digital age. Modern marketers use these tools for a wide variety of reasons such as marketing automation, customer relationship management (CRM), content management, and data and analytics. Salestech, on the other hand, is about giving salespeople the tools and insights they need to close deals and accelerate revenue growth. Salestech includes different solutions such as sales enablement, customer intelligence, and sales automation tools to help sales professionals more effectively target, engage, and win their customers, streamline processes, and drive better results.

There are many factors contributing to the rise of Martech and Salestech. One is the digital channels and touchpoints. They have expanded therefore marketers have had to adopt new tools and techniques. Secondly, customer data is becoming more and more available using new technology. Marketers now have an opportunity to use the data to gain better insights about their customers and use it to have more personalized and effective outreach. And lastly, as we have talked about numerous times in class, AI and machine learning. AI and machine learning are automating processes that a marketer used to have to carry out in the past.

The Imperative to Adapt and Leverage These Technologies

Companies today must move in the direction of embracing Martech and Salestech solutions as the digital revolution continues to grow with or without them. The facts are if they continue to do things the way they have always been done they will be left behind with the competition taking over. Leveraging Martech and Salestech can enable marketers to better know their customers, target their efforts and deliver higher impact, cost-effective growth for the company. However, simply implementing a tool or platform isn't what's going to really be the game changer in benefiting from Martech and Salestech. A cultural shift is also needed across the maturing industry that is more focused on a data-driven approach to delivering higher returns with your marketing and sales. This shift will manifest itself through breaking down the silos between departments that today still exist across many companies; it will require much greater collaboration and knowledge sharing. Additionally, the technology will continue to evolve and so will the world around them, and so as a company, they will need to be constantly testing and iterating to continue to drive high performance.

Finally, companies need to navigate the very complex and ever-evolving landscape of Martech and Salestech solutions (tools and platforms) and become experts in applying them in existing marketing and sales practices. With thousands of solutions on the market, each with its own unique value proposition and limitations, companies need to carefully evaluate and select the ones that best fit their specific needs and goals. This requires a deep knowledge of the digital ecosystem and the ability to constantly re-evaluate and change your technology stack as new solutions emerge and your business needs evolve.

Redefining Business Landscapes in the Digital Ocean

The application speed of Martech and Salestech is leading to the transformation of not just individual companies, but entire industries and their business ecosystems. This can be displayed in several different ways, including through the rise of new business models like on-demand products or services, and through the emergence of new partnership models between companies. The shift can be also through the shifting power dynamics in industries where what used to be considered emerging threats are now some of the world's most important companies. The flip side to this is that what used to be considered some of the world's most important companies become emerging threats themselves. The overall result of these forces is that industries are being mashed together in new ways. Companies such as Google and Amazon, which are known historically as tech companies, are now in industries such as healthcare, finance, and entertainment. This has blurred conventional industry boundaries.

The quick rise of Martech and Salestech shows the increasing importance of data as a strategic resource. In the digital age, companies that can effectively collect, analyze, and act on customer data will have a significant competitive advantage. This has given rise to data-driven business models, such as subscriptions and personalized recommendations that are heavily reliant on data studies of customer preferences and behaviors.

The digital revolution allows new forms of collaboration and co-creation. As companies increasingly understand the need to rapidly innovate and adapt to changing customer needs, they are also increasingly realizing the value of partnering and collaborating with others, within an industry and outside of it, to access new capabilities and refine their business models to drive growth. This means innovative partnering between incumbents and start-ups to bring new ideas to scale, as well as partnering between industries to create new value propositions and customer experiences.

Challenges and Opportunities in the Digital Ocean

While the digital ocean abounds with opportunities, old or new, it also presents serious challenges that are inherent in navigating uncharted waters. Central to these is the complexity and pace of technological change. If your business hasn't yet been significantly affected by technology, it's only a matter of time before it will be. Navigating the landscape of emerging technologies and platforms is difficult enough, but once technology is more than a peripheral part of your enterprise, the ever-accelerating rate of change will also be something with which you have to keep up.

For example, a vital challenge is balancing personalization and privacy. More data means more customer insight, but more customer insight also means you have to pay ever greater attention to gathering and using customer data, and even greater attention to the massive amounts of regulation brought in to protect customer privacy. Focusing on only one side of this equation will doom the digital marketing or sales efforts sooner or later.

The Digital Ocean also presents difficulties related to talent and organizational culture. As marketing and sales become increasingly data-driven and technology-enabled, companies must attract and retain talent with the right mix of technical and creative skills. They must also foster a culture, that is comfortable with experimentation, agility and continuous learning, and that empowers employees to challenge the status quo and embrace new technologies and ways of working. However, despite these challenges, the opportunities presented by the Digital Ocean are immense. By leveraging Martech and Salestech solutions, companies can unlock new sources of growth, efficiency, and competitive advantage. They can make customer experiences more meaningful, engaging, and persona-driven, streamline their operations and ultimately bring better business outputs.

We will now move from the iceberg to the ocean, diving deep into the worlds of Martech and Salestech. By presenting the key tools, strategies, and best practices that are needed to succeed in the digital era—and describe how these technologies are impacting marketing and sales, the author also shows you how all of these things work together to help you create and deliver seamless, attractive experiences. Finally, we will take a wider look at the digital revolution from a business and societal perspective, before providing practical insights and recommendations to help you navigate the uncharted and sometimes treacherous waters of the digital ocean.

We are at the dawn of the next great wave of innovation across all areas of our lives. We believe companies that can meld the worlds of Marketing and Sales teams to apply technology to drive innovation, growth and customer value will be the winners in the future. By acquiring the right technology, strategy and talent, and adopting that future lean-forward culture, you will not just survive the disruption sure to keep coming but thrive.

CHAPTER 2: UNDERSTANDING MARTECH AND SALESTECH

In the previous chapter, we discussed the concept of the digital ocean and how Martech (Marketing Technology) and Salestech (Sales Technology) are a critical function in helping companies navigate through this ever-changing and evolving marketplace. In this chapter we are going to study them in depth, how they evolved, what makes them upgrade, and how they are changing the game.

Evolution of Martech and Salestech and Their Key Components

Martech and Salestech emerged from the early days of digital marketing and sales technologies when companies began deploying email marketing, CRM systems, and other assortments of tools to engage customers and improve their sales processes. But it is only within the past decade that these technologies have begun to truly mature, driven by the advance of cloud computing, big data analytics, and artificial intelligence.

Today, the Martech and Salestech landscape is vast and complex, covering thousands of tools and platforms across a wide range of categories. Some of the key components of Martech include:

1. An app(s) to help marketers automate repetitive actions like e-mail marketing, social media posting, and, in turn, generating leads for a business. This is very instrumental when scaling out, because it takes repetitive work off the hands of employees, and makes marketing more efficient. These apps often come with automated workflows, lead scoring models, and campaign frameworks, which are instrumental for

marketers to send and track relevant messages to customers at scale.

2. Content Management Systems (CMS): Applications that allow users to create, edit, organize, and publish digital content. CMSs are generally used to avoid the necessity of hand-coding a website every time there needs to be a content update. They can be used for storing, controlling, versioning, and publishing industry-specific documentation such as news articles, operators' manuals, technical manuals, sales templates, design templates, marketing assets and a variety of other types of documents. CMSs vary widely in their complexity and ease of use. As a website, words in a CMS document can be mapped to a structured and styled template. Once mapped, the resulting document is treated as an HTML document.

3. CRM (Customer Relationship Manager): A type of software that helps companies track and analyze their interactions with clients to improve sales and business partnerships. Most CRM vendors like Salesforce, Microsoft, and ACT! provide features for contact management, lead management, opportunity management and customer service. Some vendors also offer analytics and reporting features that can help companies gain insights into their customer base.

4. Data Analysis and Business Intelligence: These are tools that let marketers collect, analyze, and interpret data. They help you ask the right questions of your data, and help determine which answers could be of greatest benefit to your organization. Many have dashboards and reporting capabilities to help you visualize and interpret the data you've already collected. These tools generally focus on data integration (extracting data from various sources) data warehousing (storing and managing data from many sources) and data mining (analyzing the data to find patterns or correlations).

5. Personalization and Optimization: Tools that help marketers test variables in the marketing mix to improve accuracy and efficiency. Machine learning and predictive analytics also fall into this category and are very useful for analyzing data and

using that data to make recommendations and offers to customers in real time. Examples: personalized email campaigns, product recommendations, and personalized website content.

On the Salestech side, some of the key components are:

1. Sales Enablement: The objective is to provide sales teams with the content, tools, training, and analytics they need to optimize sales coordination and to successfully engage with prospective buyers throughout the buying process. Basically, it's so they can sell more easily! The foundation of the sales enablement is to provide Sales with what they need to be successful in – you guessed it – selling! Whether that's collateral, training, or the latest competitive analysis, the job of the sales enablement provider is to make the sales enablement process as easy as possible.
2. Tools that help sales teams find context about their customers and prospects in order to better sell to them. This includes audience demographics, competitive intelligence, and other information that might help a sales rep get their foot in the door or expand into an established relationship. This information can often be aggregated from multiple sources, such as social media, public records and proprietary databases to give sales reps a full, 360-degree look at their customers and create a personalized sales approach.
3. Sales Automation: The Sales Department uses different tools that help them improve their work. Sales Automation types of tools allow your sales team to streamline and automate repetitive, manual processes like lead routing, contract management, and order processing, or any selling process. The Sales team uses, for example, configuration pricing and quoting (CPQ) software to expedite the creation of customer quotes and sales proposals. Sales automation tools also include potent integrations with CPQ, e-signature, contract management, and other back-office tools.
4. Configure, price, quote (CPQ): Software tools that help sales teams quickly and accurately generate quotes for orders. The

tools can include sources for configuration, recommendations for pricing and help in generating the quote or proposal, and can often be a part of a complete suite of sales acceleration tools. CPQ tools typically include pricing features, cost/quote and discount calculators, quote creation tools and integrations with CRM, ERP and sometimes, CPQ can handle renewals, upgrades, and add-ons.
5. Partner Relationship Management (PRM): a system of methodologies, strategies, software, and web-based capabilities that help a vendor manage partner relationships. PRM is not just an IT solution, but a strategic approach to generally managing the partner relationship.

As the Martech and Salestech landscapes have matured and expanded, the two have become increasingly intertwined, with many tools and platforms spanning multiple categories and use cases. For example, a marketing automation platform may also include capabilities for content management, personalization, and analytics whereas a sales enablement platform might feature tools for content creation, customer intelligence, and performance tracking.

The confusion of boundaries between Martech and Salestech reflects the growing realization that marketing and sales are interdependent: Two sides of the same coin working together to drive customer engagement and revenue growth. By leveraging the right mix of tools and platforms across both, companies can deliver a continuous (and persuasive) customer experience that drives business results.

Convergence of Marketing, Sales, and Technology

One of the more pronounced trends in the evolution of Martech and Salestech is the growing overlap between marketing, sales, and technology. Although in the past, there existed functional silos between these areas, collaboration and integration concerning these functions were limited. In the digital era, however, the walls are fast crumbling down.

Several factors are driving this convergence. First and foremost, the proliferation of digital channels and touchpoints has created a need for more seamless and integrated customer experiences across the entire customer journey. Customers today expect consistent experiences with brands across all channels, from social media and email to websites and mobile apps, meaning close collaboration between marketing, sales and technology (the Martech triumvirate) is more important than ever. It's a case of bringing the right message, to the right person, at the right time, in the right place.

Education is the second major element that marketers must address. The advent of big data has provided marketers with a wealth of customer data that didn't exist before. Companies can now see what customers are doing, discussing, thinking, and feeling in an unprecedented manner. This sounds great, but as Kelly explained, these data are not efficiently organized in most firms. Marketers must collaborate closely with their sales counterparts to transform data into insights and insights into results. Marketers need to dive into data in greater detail to identify trends, develop campaigns in collaboration with sales, and measure results.

Lastly, the immediacy of the market requires more agile and adaptive marketing and sales interventions. Technology transforms so quickly and the demands of the consumer seem to change in no time at all. The marketing and sales teams need to react very quickly to consumer demands, they need to constantly change their marketing or sales approach and techniques catering to the changes that happen in the marketing place. This needs a steady pulse on the ever-evolving technology landscape and the ability to adapt and apply the latest tools and platforms to their marketing and sales workflows.

This convergence is giving rise to new roles and functions at the intersection of marketing, sales, and technology. For example, many companies now have Chief Revenue Officers (CROs) who own the ultimate number and are responsible for driving growth across both marketing and sales. Similarly, Chief Marketing Technologists (CMTs) have emerged as a new breed of marketing executives, given by Gartner the self-explanatory name: "marketing technology tool and process experts and infusers." Sales enablement has emerged as a new, cross-functional discipline that helps ensure marketing and sales are aligned around the same goals: to engage with, sell to, and retain the best customers. As Gartner explains, the chief sales enablement officer's role is "to lead the planning and execution of all sales enablement activities, and to provide communication, coordination and collaboration between all stakeholders in the sales enablement charter."

Other key roles emerging in the marketing organization of the future include data scientists, who will help companies organize and make sense of the vast amounts of customer data they collect, and customer experience (CX) specialists, who will be responsible for designing and delivering a seamless, personalized customer experience across all touchpoints. These roles reflect the fact that driving growth in the digital age requires a multidisciplinary approach that spans marketing, sales, technology, and beyond.

Empowering Data-Driven Decision-Making

Martech and Salestech, when utilized properly, can empower data-driven decision-making. In the digital age, companies have more access to customer data than ever before. Websites, social media, sensors, CRM and transaction databases are all sources of customer data. This data is only useful when it is collected efficiently, analyzed accurately and acted upon. The beauty of Martech and Salestech is that they provide the tools and platforms to take customer data and make it actionable. Martech and Salestech allow marketers and salespeople to turn customer data into insights. Marketing automation platforms, for example, can track all of the touch points a prospect or customer has and display them in the same spot. Marketers can then use this data to optimize campaigns, improving overall marketing performance.

The same goes for sales intelligence tools, which can allow sales teams to know what leads to going after, such as if the company fits a particular mold (e.g. enterprise-scale, healthcare industry) or if they've engaged with the brand before – that way sales reps can go after the leads most likely to convert to cut down on inefficiency and drive a faster sales cycle.

Of course, enabling data-driven decision-making requires technology – but it also requires a cultural shift within the organization. Data and analytics need to be valued as critical drivers of business success. That means tearing down data silos, fostering collaboration between functions, and investing in the skills needed to understand and apply the insights pulled from data.

Data strategy is about creating a holistic view of how data can help deliver on your business objectives. It looks at the entire organization's data-related needs: not just your immediate business goals, but the entire set of objectives for the company. It considers the information you need to achieve those objectives, where you can get it, and how you're going to turn that into action. As a reminder, anything that is not directly linked to how the information will impact your business objectives is irrelevant. A data strategy should be treated as a living document; something that is constantly reviewed and updated as technology changes or the business evolves.

This is all on the condition, that the company already has the infrastructure and the systems in place, that can be used for the data gathering and for using it to find out the different outputs – like finding the outliers, finding where the best source is of a certain lead or other possible uses – in other words, if all the systems and procedures are set up to use the data to find out what it was supposed to be used for (when it was put in, gathered and stored).

Both Martech and Salestech can help a company make better decisions by using the data of their customers to optimize the marketing and sell It is important to note that not all companies are ready to embrace the data and analytics revolution. The use of both Martech and Salestech requires a fundamental belief that data and analytics are an essential part of doing business. It also requires the right tools, the right processes, and the right people to not only capture data but to analyze it and make informed decisions based on what you learn.

The Evolving Role of Technology in Business Growth

As Martech and Salestech advanced and became more mature it's transforming the role of technology in organizations as a business growth driver, not just a support function, now it's actually a strategic enabler of marketing and sales success. Technology now allows you to engage customers, automate processes, and gain insights more effectively, you can drive incremental revenue from existing customers at marginal incremental cost. This has a profound impact on how companies do marketing and sales and it changes the skill sets and competence required for success in marketing and sales. Marketers have to master not only the traditional skills of creativity, communication & relationship building but also become competent in data analysis, technology management, digital strategy, etc.

Additionally, the increased importance of technology in sales and marketing is causing a greater need for IT to collaborate and align more closely with other departments in the business. Now the marketing and sales departments are working with IT to make sure that they have the correct technology and infrastructure. It is no longer an order taker or the department that should just say now. They are saying yes how would you like us to do it and how can we afford it?

On the horizon, the utilization of technology to grow business will only continue to evolve. New capabilities that are emerging such as machine learning, AI, and IoT will provide additional opportunities for marketing and sales innovation. For instance, chatbots and virtual assistants powered by AI can increase the scalability of customer service & support organizations, and predictive analytics can help guide sales professionals to uncover the best opportunities and how best to pursue them.

The fast pace of technological change introduces additional challenges for companies. New tools and platforms seem to emerge every other day, so how do you know which technologies are worth the investment? And how do you integrate them into your existing processes and workflows? This requires a deep understanding of the technology landscape, of course, as well as a willingness to experiment and take calculated risks. We also have to think about innovation, experimentation and the general business organization and structures: To succeed in this environment, companies must foster a culture of innovation and agility. This means valuing experimentation, learning, and continuous improvement and also making sure that you have the right talent and capabilities in place.

As time goes on the role of technology as a part of driving business growth will only continue to evolve. The smart companies that can align themselves with the technologies and find innovative ways to drive revenue (Martech) and use technology to enable the sales team to drive revenue (Salestech) will be the ones that will continue to reign and grow in the digital age.

In the chapters ahead, we'll dive deeper into how exactly Martech and Salestech can be used to achieve specific business outcomes. First, we'll explain briefly how these technologies can be used specifically to improve customer experiences and increase the ROIs of marketing activities. Second, we'll assess the effective ways Martech and Salestech can be leveraged to boost sales productivity and drive revenue growth. Finally, we'll demonstrate the key challenges and considerations when it comes to implementing and integrating these technologies, and more importantly, some best practices for success. With these insights, you'll not only have a concrete understanding of just how exactly Martech and Salestech can help fuel business growth online and offline but also a process to achieve your own marketing and sales objectives with these technologies.

CHAPTER 3: LEVERAGING MARTECH FOR MARKETING SUCCESS

In the last chapter, we covered the history and key components of Martech and Salestech, as well as the convergence of marketing, sales and technology which is enabling data-driven decision making and changing the role of technology in driving business. In this chapter, we will take this discussion further to learn how Martech can be put to use to drive marketing success, whether your focus is on improving marketing ROI or enhancing customer experiences.

Enhancing Customer Experience, Personalization, and Engagement with Martech

One of the key benefits of Martech is its ability to enhance customer experience, personalization, and engagement. In today's digital age, customers expect personalized, relevant, and timely interactions with brands across all channels and touchpoints. Martech provides the tools and platforms needed to deliver on these expectations and create more meaningful and engaging customer experiences.

Marketing automation platforms can aid companies in transmitting the exact personalized message to customers based on their behavior logs and preferences. Tracking customers on all kinds of touchpoints assists in getting a complete vision of customers' journey to deliver the right message, at the right time, to the right customer through the right media which is highly impossible without the technology.

Additionally, many companies are using personalization engines, which help to make the experience on a company's website or mobile app more individual based on the users' previous interactions or behavior on a site. These engines can take all sorts of data like previous search histories, page views and purchase history to suggest products, content, or offers that are tailored exactly to that user.

Another example of Martech tools that could potentially be utilized is customer feedback and survey platforms. These tools could be imperative in obtaining real-time customer insights, testing new ideas and products, building a targeted customer experience to match the targeted market, and collecting in-depth data and feedback.

From Lead Generation to Nurturing & Conversion with Marketing Automation

Martech can also help expedite and automate the lead generation, nurturing and conversion processes. Marketing automation platforms, in particular, have completely transformed these critical marketing functions. Marketing automation can help companies attract and capture leads from countless online sources, often through various email, social and, website forms including, general contact, newsletter subscription, content download, and the like. By creating and producing custom, piece-specific content and promotions, on the proper platform, companies can reach and engage their targeted prospects effectively and ensure the correct, intended leads end up in the sales funnel. It is imperative to note that, companies must engage in a lead attribution before entering any Martech campaign. Martech helps companies nurture leads through the funnel more quickly. With proper marketing automation, companies can further engage their leads throughout the sales process with precision-targeted, timely, relevant content and promotions. By breaking down leads by their behaviors, preferences, and interests, companies can deliver just the right message to their target audience at each stage of their unique buyer's journey. Good nurturing will help usher leads through the sales cycle more smoothly and shorten the conversion time.

Additionally, marketing automation can be used to customize the journey that a lead takes through your marketing funnel. when a new lead first lands on your website or interacts with your brand for the first time at the very top of your funnel they may not be very detailed and informed about what your company does and how your product or service can help solve their problems. You can use marketing automation to send a series of emails following the initial interaction to give your lead more info about your product or service. As the lead continues to engage with the content, indicating more and more interest in your product or service you can also begin to target the emails you send your lead with more specific offers or promotions to move them along the sales process. Finally, marketing automation can be used to help companies score and prioritize leads based on what actions the lead has taken and how likely they are to convert. Factors such as email opens, clicks, website visits, and form submissions can be used to create a lead score for each of your prospects to help your sales team know who they should be spending their time following up with.

Creating Content That Converts Across the Sales Funnel

When it comes to effectively leveraging Martech for lead generation, nurturing, and conversion, companies must ensure they are creating content that resonates with their target market and drives action at various stages throughout the funnel.

Top of the funnel is all about attracting and engaging potential customers. You want to create content that answers questions your target market may have about their current challenge or goal. A few formats of content that are commonly used to engage and attract visitors are blog posts, social media updates, infographics, and educational or entertaining content that does not sell. The purpose of top-of-funnel content is to provide value to the reader and bring awareness that your brand exists.

The further leads move down the funnel, the more targeted and action-oriented content should become. These leads need more information on the benefits of the product/service and also need some sort of motivation to convert. This could include case studies, demos, free trials, limited-time offers, and incentives that create a sense of urgency and encourage action.

To create killer content for each stage, you're going to need to do some serious channeling of the audience. To do this, really dig deep into user personas and develop a solid understanding of the types of people that are most likely to become customers. Where are they on the Internet? What kind of content makes them click? What do they get out of converting? What information do they need at each stage of the funnel? This will require some heavy lifting between the marketing and sales teams. Give your role to someone skilled and knowledgeable who can achieve your desired end results. Use hard data, analytics, and other metrics to steer your content development strategy. What works? What doesn't? Why does it work? How can you do it better?

Content Strategy for Different Buyers

Another consideration for companies looking to create content for the different stages in the sales funnel is the different types of buyers that are targeted. A content strategist must create good content that will resonate with the different audiences.

So, in the example above, where the B2B company is selling enterprise software, ideally the company would want to create content that would appeal to both the technical buyer as well as the business buyer. With a technical buyer being an IT manager or developer, ideally, the content strategy should focus on detailed product specifications, case studies, and technical whitepapers. On the other hand, a business buyer (executives, department heads, etc.) could focus more on the strategic benefits of the solution; again, this would be content that could answer questions such as: Can this truly reduce my overall costs? How exactly is this going to make us more efficient? Will this significantly increase my competitive advantage?

A B2C company that sells consumer products may have buyer personas with an entirely different set of needs, preferences, and values. For example, consumers might be busy moms, fitness enthusiasts, or eco-conscious consumers, each with very different reasons for buying and specific content needs. To reach these consumers, the company may need to have completely different content strategies. For each buyer persona, the B2C company above creates, such as busy moms, fitness enthusiasts, and eco-conscious consumers, the firm needs to apply unique content strategies to meet different buyer needs, preferences, and values. The typical approach to building buyer personas is to develop a set of interview questions for the different types of buyers who are very likely to purchase your product(s) or service(s). The goal of the interviews is for the interviewees to talk you through a recent purchase they made like the one your buying personas are typically responsible for. Many companies will develop a list of 5-10 information needs they would like to obtain from the interviewee. Once you have conducted multiple interviews (somewhere between 10-15), the firm can begin the research and develop a few primary buying personas. The firm should then develop a primary problem(s) for each of the segments, 3-4 primary needs, 2-3 preferences, and a primary value sought.

Leveraging Martech Tools for Effective Content Distribution

Once companies develop a content strategy, create content, and have it tagged appropriately for content stage and persona organizations must now use their Martech stacks to distribute content effectively. Martech allows companies to reach and engage target audiences across multiple channels and touchpoints which is one of the main benefits of Martech. Some of the best Martech tools for distribution include:

1. Email marketing platforms: These tools automate the process of sending targeted, personalized emails to subscribers based on predefined parameters, such as trigger events and preferences.
2. Social media management platforms: These tools facilitate the planning, scheduling, and posting of content across multiple social media channels, as well as real-time tracking and interaction with social media mentions and conversations.
3. Content management systems (CMS): These platforms allow businesses to create, edit, and publish a variety of content

types, such as blog and website articles, landing page layouts, multimedia files, and image galleries.
4. Paid advertising platforms: These tools enable companies to promote their content to a highly-targeted audience through pay-per-click (PPC) text, display, and video ads, as well as sponsored updates and posts.

Effectively differentiating and communicating what your brand does, what it stands for, and the values it represents can be a daunting task. Nevertheless, doing so is imperative to ensure your brand image is in line with your brand promise. Thankfully, thanks to a host of Martech tools, brands now have at their disposal the necessary means to distribute their content to their target audience, at the right time. The right kind of content has the potential to raise brand awareness and generate more traffic, increase engagement, and hence more conversions.

Moreover, businesses must ensure that they are using each tool to meet and engage the target market. Implementing these tools is not enough. Companies must have a plan and strategy in place on how they are going to use the tools that are given. This includes setting goals and KPIs for each channel and have a content calendar and publishing schedule. Companies must also continuously monitor and optimize performance based on data and analytics, so companies can be successful. In today's fast-paced marketplace, companies must also have tools and platforms in place to enhance customer experience, and automate lead generation and nurturing so companies can drive conversions by effectively creating and distributing content. By employing Martech and having a content strategy specifically aligned to the target audience's needs and preferences, companies can drive significant improvements in marketing performance and ROI.

However, just having the right tools is not enough to successfully implement and integrate Martech solutions. It also requires a strategy to be executed, tight alignment between marketing and sales teams, and a continued commitment to optimization and improvement with your data and insights. Coming up next in Chapter 14, we explore how to further drive marketing and sales performance and business growth with Salestech.

CHAPTER 4: EMPOWERING SALES WITH SALESTECH

In the previous chapter, we discussed Martech and how it can be used to deliver great customer experiences, automate lead generation and nurturing, and improve revenue through content creation and outreach. In this chapter, our attention will be on Salestech. How can we use the technology to empower sales teams, improve overall sales performance, and drive better revenue?

Sales Enablement: Empowering Your Sales Team

Sales Enablement is a popular term in the Salestech arena. It refers to any startup that gives your sales team the ability to work better. This includes things like helping the reps find leads, as well as tools that they can use while closing the lead. You get the idea. These startups have grown significantly in popularity for the simple reason that they streamline an otherwise chaotic process.

Central to many of these platforms is the idea of a Cloud for sales content, with sales decks, case studies, product demos, and marketing literature being made available to sales reps, giving them what they need to educate and persuade prospective customers. When companies invest in content, and provide their sales reps with a cloud full of up-to-date, valuable, and curated content, made to close deals.

Sales enablement platforms also offer a plethora of additional tools and resources such as training & coaching, sales performance tracking & analytics, and CRM & marketing automation integrations to name a few. Consequently, Sales Enablement Platforms can also assist in onboarding and training new sales reps more quickly, identify and help address gaps in sales rep or sales process performance, and continuously improve sales processes and outcomes.

Sales Intelligence: Knowing Your Customers Before They Know You

Sales reps can also use Salestech for deeper insight into their customers and prospects resulting in a more tailored approach and messaging to every buyer. With the help of sales intelligence tools like lead enrichment and buyer intent data platforms, sales reps can collect and analyze data on prospective customers before they engage with them. Lead enrichment tools aid the sales team in filling in missing or incomplete information on leads – this could include company size, the industry they work in, job title, or key contacts). By helping sales reps to build up as complete a picture of each lead as possible, lead enrichment tools can help sales reps determine which leads they should devote their time to engaging with, as well as curating their messaging to each prospect's unique needs and challenges.

Buyer intent data platforms let you know that customers have been actively researching the types of products or services that you sell. These platforms just don't scrape the websites that visitors are going to they pull in data from search engines, review sites, and social media platforms to tell you which companies are most likely to be in-market for a solution like the one you provide. The benefit of this is that you have the ability to focus your sales efforts on the people who should be more interested in buying from you.

Using Sales Automation Tools to Streamline Processes

Salestech can also streamline and automate various sales processes, from lead routing and assignment to contract management and invoicing. Sales automation tools like customer relationship management (CRM) and configure price, and quote (CPQ) software save companies time and reduce errors by taking over repetitive manual activities. They also help these companies preserve the rich, intimate data that is the lifeblood of the sales function. A CRM platform, for example, might automatically route fresh leads to the appropriate sales rep based on the subset of factors that are likely to most influence conversion probability, such as geography, industry, and company size. It might also nudge the rep to optimize conversion by, say, following up the next day with a personal thank-you note or scheduling a check-in call with the lead six days hence.

CPQ software, on the other hand, helps sales reps generate quotes and proposals quickly and accurately based on pre-defined pricing and discount rules. By automating the quoting process, these tools can also help reduce errors and inconsistencies and speed up the sales cycle by eliminating manual calculations and approvals. Other types of sales automation tools that can be useful toward the final stages of the sales process include e-signature and contract management software. Using e-signature software helps users send contracts for a quick and easy fill-out and electronic signing. Users are also able to house all signed contracts in the systems contract management outlook.

Building High-Performing Sales Teams in the Digital Age

Though sales tech can help, companies should remember that technology isn't the only thing you need to get the most out of your sales team. To truly succeed in the digital age, companies must also focus on the skills, knowledge, and mindset of their sales teams. Companies must invest in ongoing training and coaching to help their sales reps leverage the data and insights surfaced by sales tech. Reps should receive training on product updates, industry trends, best practices for selling and communication, to name a few. Secondly, companies must cultivate a culture of ongoing learning and improvement. reps should be encouraged to try new things, share best practices, and learn from both their successes and failures.

Additionally, building high-performing sales teams requires strong leadership and cross-functional partnerships between Sales and other functions like Marketing, Customer Success and Product Development. Sales Leaders need to set goals and expectations, provide consistent feedback and recognition, and create an environment where their teams feel supported and empowered.

Virtual and Augmented Reality in Sales

One emerging area of Salestech that has the potential to revolutionize the sales process is virtual reality (VR) and augmented reality (AR). VR and AR allow salespeople to create immersive, interactive experiences for prospective customers, in person or at a distance. For example, a company that sells a complex piece of industrial equipment can use VR to show customers a virtual tour of their factory as well as how the equipment works in an actual real-world setting instead of just showing a customer a brochure with a fancy picture of the equipment. Or a seller of furniture can use AR to allow the customer to see what a certain piece of furniture would actually look like in the customer's house before the customer buys the furniture.

Virtual and augmented reality can make the sales experience more engaging and more memorable, thus better positioning the brand against its competitors and building stronger relationships with potential customers. VR and AR can also help the sales representative explain the value and benefits of their product or service—particularly if it's a complex or intangible offering. Nonetheless, implementing VR and AR in sales requires a significant investment in technology and training. You must have sales reps who are comfortable using these electronic tools, and you must have the infrastructure and support to create and deliver high-quality VR and AR experiences.

To conclude, Salestech offers a wide variety of tools and platforms that can help sales teams significantly. Some of these include sales enablement, sales techniques, sales automation, and VR. Ultimately, sales teams which leverage these technologies and develop the skills and mindset of their sales team will see an uptick in sales performance, revenue growth, and stronger relationships with their customers.

But the important task when hiring these types of Salestech tools is the implementation and the integration. How can we do this effectively and efficiently, what are the necessary ingredients required from the set menu and from the a la carte menu? A clear strategy is required, and this is true of any technology investment; excellent alignment will be required between sales and other functions across the organization. Continuous learning and improvement is also a must because your tech will become outdated in a few years.

CHAPTER 5: INTEGRATING MARTECH AND SALESTECH

In the previous chapters, we talked about how you can use Martech and Salestech. It is really important to use these technologies together and seamlessly. Martech and Salestech are super useful and can work extremely well, but to obtain maximum value, your company really needs to have them integrated into your business.

Bridging the Gap Between Marketing and Sales Through Technology

Another major benefit of Martech integration with Salestech is that it helps to close the gap between the marketing and sales teams, creating a more coordinated and customer-centric approach to delivering revenue. Marketing and sales have traditionally operated in very different silos, with different objectives, different metrics, different technologies and little integration, which leads to an inconsistent customer experience, increased duplication of effort, and missed opportunities for collaboration and optimization.

Integrating Salestech and Martech systems will aid in breaking down silos that occur, and create a much better-flowing system of information from marketing to sales. A few examples of this could be integrating a marketing automation platform with a CRM system, which would allow the marketing team to automatically pass along any qualified leads straight to the sales teams and it would also give them the correct date in which is needed to close a sale. Another example could be, integrating a sales enablement platform with a content management system, so that if there are any new features on a product, the sales team will automatically be sent an email and it will also be uploaded to their dashboard, therefore they will be able to have the most up to date and relevant information available for the next time they speak to their prospects.

Aligning Martech and Salestech for Seamless Integration

An essential first step for companies to successfully integrate Martech and Salestech systems is to align marketing and sales teams around shared goals, metrics, and processes. This requires strong leadership and communication from both marketing and sales leaders to challenge existing silos and ways of working. One effective approach is to create a shared revenue operations (DevOps) function that sits at the intersection of marketing, sales, and customer success. DevOps teams are responsible for managing the customer journey from identification and acquisition to retention and growth. They work closely with both marketing and sales to ensure all systems, processes, and data are in sync to drive maximum revenue impact.

Another crucial element in Martech and Salestech Alignment is making sure that data can be consistently and conveniently accessed through all systems. This implies the need for a well-defined data strategy and appropriate governance model along with reliable data integration and management tools. Data may only be useful to companies if it can be trusted to be accurate and complete and conveniently accessed and analyzed for insights and decision-making.

Achieving a Unified View of the Customer Journey

Unifying the customer journey, from awareness and engagement to sell-through and post-sale support, is one of the ultimate goals of integrating Martech and Salestech. By combining data from multiple touchpoints and systems, companies can get a single, more complete, and more accurate view of each individual customer's needs, preferences, and behaviors.

As an example, integrating website analytics data with CRM data can show what pages individual prospects have visited, or what content they've downloaded from the site. That data can then be used to personalize the sales outreach and tailor the messaging since it's a known fact that the prospect has an expressed interest in those topics. Similarly, integrating customer support/feedback data with sales data can show where the customer may be in the decision-making process. That data can be used to identify opportunities for cross- and up-sell, or proactively address any issues or concerns that may impact customer satisfaction and/or retention.

Getting to this kind of unified view of the customer journey is not just a matter of having integrated systems and data. Besides that, you also have to have the right kind of mindset and culture within your organization. Your teams have to be incented and have the power to share and collaborate across functions, always making sure the customer's needs and experience are at the center of all decisions.

Strategies for Data Sharing, Lead Management, and Closed-Loop Reporting

For companies to take advantage of this unified view of the customer journey with their IA platform, they must also develop data-sharing strategies, lead management, and closed-loop reporting between marketing and sales.

How well did our past sales leads perform, and which types should we focus on to drive business? To answer these questions, marketing, and sales must create a shared definition of a "qualified lead," implement a scalable lead management process, and establish a closed-loop process with sales to report on the quality of the leads that are being handed over.

Once leads are passed to sales, sales should provide regular feedback about progress and outcomes. Sales teams should provide updates on lead status, how many leads they've converted, revenue generated from each lead and any useful information about the quality of those leads that will help marketing improve their campaigns and content. Marketing also wants to look at long-term lead performance and show how leads closed as customers measure up against their non-closed counterparts with respect to revenue, customer lifetime value or any other key attribute. Closed-loop reporting - reporting through which both teams can see the entire closed loop of information in one report - is a critical tool. It allows marketing and sales to understand the direct result of each team's efforts on revenue, customer acquisition, and a range of related outcomes.

Depending on your company's systems, processes and organizational structure, your strategy for sharing data and managing leads will differ. However, here are some best practices that are common across the board:

1. Build a centralized data repository or customer data platform (CDP) that can integrate and normalize data from different sources;
2. Develop a lead scoring and routing tool that can automatically evaluate and assign leads based on predefined criteria;
3. Implement standardized lead handoff, and follow-up procedure, with clear roles and responsibilities of each involved team in the lead management process;
4. Conduct regular pipeline review and performance tracking meetings to show what has been working positively, share insights, and identify opportunities for improvement.

By incorporating the process, tactics and tools, the business practice would turn into the knowledge and experience nurturing leads that align better and gain greater results in both the sales and marketing sectors. The important fact to remember when it comes to the topic of integrating Martech and Salestech is that it isn't a one-and-done project. This process should constantly be analyzed, reevaluated, and adjusted when necessary. As the customer changes and adjusts their expectations and needs, and as new technology advances change our lives, being able to quickly change and respond to these adjustments is crucial to thrive.

The iteration builds a culture of experimentation and learning, and a willingness to challenge existing processes and ways of working. It will also require strong leadership and cross-functional collaboration, with a shared commitment to putting the customer at the heart of every decision. By successfully integrating their Martech and Salestech systems and processes, ambitious corporations can create a more seamless, personalized and effective end-to-end customer experience that ultimately delivers long-term growth and profitability. In the next chapter, we will look at a more comprehensive Martech and Salestech ecosystem and how to navigate this increasingly complex landscape to identify the right solutions for your business.

CHAPTER 6: NAVIGATING THE DIGITAL ECOSYSTEM

In the previous chapter, we saw the importance of having a seamless operation between the Martech and Salestech systems. In this chapter, we will be learning the bigger picture of marketing and sales technologies, the tools and platforms and how you can make it all come together and be a success in the digital age.

Understanding the Complex Digital Ecosystem and Its Components

The digital ecosystem is a complex and ever-evolving landscape, encompassing a wide range of technologies, platforms, and services. At a high level, this ecosystem can be broken down into several key categories:

1. Martech – As we've learned, Martech covers a wide range of technologies and platforms aimed at improving business outcomes through marketing activities, including content management, social media management, analytics, and marketing automation, among other tools and approaches.
2. Salestech: Sales technologies, or Salestech, span the portal for DSRP Platforms within the broader revenue tech landscape. Enter Salestech - a term SaleScout is not included to refer some of the technologies and platforms that refer to sales activity like CRM - Customer Relationship Management, Sales Enablement, Revenue Operations to name a few.
3. Adtech is short for advertising technology. It refers to different types of technologies and platforms used within the context of advertising. Adtech can refer to technologies used in advertising like programmatic advertising and demand-side platforms. It can also refer to the companies that create those

technologies, like ad networks, advertising agencies, and marketing automation companies.
4. Digital Commerce: This segment essentially consists of technologies and platforms used to enable the purchase of goods and services online. Examples include e-commerce platforms, payment gateways, and fraud detection software.
5. Customer data platforms (CDPs): An infrastructure that collects, integrates and activates data from various first-, second-, and third-party sources to achieve a single customer view, making it easier and more efficient to personalize and optimize marketing and sales initiatives.
6. Cloud computing and storage: Cloud providers, like Amazon Web Services (AWS), Google Cloud and Microsoft Azure are providing the infrastructure and services to operate and scale your digital operations.
7. Artificial intelligence and machine learning: Use AI and ML technologies such as natural language processing (NLP), computer vision, and predictive analytics to automate and optimize prospecting, lead generation, segmentation, forecasting, recommendation, content marketing, social media marketing, pricing, and sales process.

These categories include many vendors, services, and products, many of which are constantly evolving and/or entering the market. Keeping up with all of them is a challenge, particularly for advertisers who are relatively new to building out digital capabilities.

Key Trends in Martech & Salestech

To make sense of the digital ecosystem to our readers, it's important to stay on top of the latest trends and developments in Martech and Salestech. Some of the key trends disrupting even forming the landscape today include:

1. In earlier chapters, we mentioned there is convergence and consolidation, companies are often looking for more of an

integrated look in their marketing or sales technologies, looking for a more seamless experience for their customer.
2. AI and Automation: AI and machine learning are being used to automate and optimize more and more marketing and sales tasks from lead scoring and nurturing to more personalized content and product recommendations.
3. Another way to personalize the interaction with a lead is Account-based marketing (ABM). ABM focuses on the target account or company as a whole, not one individual lead/contact (Marcus Andrews, 2015). ABM is a strategy that requires deep collaboration and involvement from the sales and marketing team as well as access to special data and technology.
4. Privacy and data governance: With the increasing prevalence of data breaches and consumer data misuse, companies are making data governance and your customers' privacy and security top priorities.
5. The primary driving force is the customer experience which, has continued to increase due to customer's expectations. With the customer's expectations, the company uses technology, platforms, etc. which can promote them in achieving more personalized, reliable and seamless experiences by all channels and touchpoints.
6. Sales enablement tools – the highlight of this article. Tools like sales content management, training and coaching, and performance analytics are making it easier for companies to shorten the sales cycle and close deals faster.

By staying on top of these and other trends, companies can make more informed decisions about which technologies and platforms to invest in, and how to integrate them into their overall marketing and sales strategies.

Identifying Key Players and Trends Shaping the Digital Landscape

Another key aspect of navigating the digital ecosystem is identifying the major players and vendors shaping the landscape. Some of the most prominent and influential players in Martech and Salestech today:

1. Salesforce, previously known as Data.com, is one of the largest CRM and sales enablement platforms out there and boasts an impressive clientele including Coca-Cola, ADP and Western Union. It encompasses a large suite of tools and services pertaining to sales, marketing and customer service as well.
2. Adobe has an amazing list of analytics and marketing tools that they offer. They have the Adobe Experience Cloud available that offers solutions for content, personalization, advertising, and analytics.
3. Oracle provides a variety of different marketing and sales technologies that their company uses such as the Oracle Marketing Cloud and Oracle Sales Cloud as well as their customer data platform, Oracle Unity.
4. HubSpot is one of the most popular marketing automation and CRM platforms. HubSpot is an all-in-one marketing automation platform that offers user-friendly tools for email marketing campaigns, blogging, social media, Search Engine Optimization (SEO), building websites, creating landing pages, other web marketing tools, lead nurturing, CRM and includes big libraries of tutorial videos and a massive knowledge base.
5. Owned by Adobe, Marketo is a marketing automation platform that includes lead management, email marketing, consumer and mobile marketing, customer base marketing, and account-based marketing.
6. Google offers an array of advertising and analytics tools like Google Ads, Google Analytics, and Google Marketing Platform.
7. LinkedIn is a business-focused platform that has more than 500 million members. It is a marketing and sales tool designed for companies to target professional audiences based on what industry they work in, their job function, their work experience, where they went to school, what they are skilled

in, their geographic location, what they click on, what they buy, and by company. Some of LinkedIn's marketing and sales tools include LinkedIn Marketing Solutions and LinkedIn Sales Navigator.

The examples above are just a few vendors and platforms in the Martech and Salestech space. There are many vendors and platforms your company may want to consider, but the 'right' vendors for your company will depend on your company's specific needs and requirements. When evaluating vendors look at the solutions they offer, their pricing, and integrations as well as how well the vendor and platform fit with your company's strategy and goals.

Achieving this level of data integration requires a deep understanding of marketing and sales processes and deep access to the customer data and the technology infrastructure of the company. It also requires complex system development and close collaboration between the marketing and sales functions and the IT team to ensure that new technologies and platforms are correctly integrated into existing routing and workflow in marketing.

Companies should also be tuned to the evolving digital landscape, watching out for new technologies and platforms, as well as shifts in customer behavior and expectations. Examples of these changes include the rise of voice assistants and smart speakers, which is giving rise to new ways to engage customers and deliver content through voice interfaces, and the growing popularity of messaging apps and chatbots, which are changing how companies deliver real-time customer service and engage with their audiences. The increasing importance of video and visual content is also driving demand for new ways to create, manage, and distribute that content.

Companies need to monitor trends, technology, and evaluate their marketing, and sales channels to stay competitive in a fast-changing consumer-driven marketplace. However effectively managing the digital ecosystem is about more than just technology. It requires the right foundation of strategy, process, and people. The next section of this guide will address various strategic challenges and considerations to successfully build and execute digitally transformative strategies and how Martech in concert with Salestech can support this execution in substantive ways.

CHAPTER 7: CHALLENGES IN DIGITAL TRANSFORMATION

As we have already learned, many companies are in the throes of a complex digital ecosystem and navigating the Martech and Salestech landscape is no easy feat. In fact, this is one of the biggest challenges organizations face when it comes to digital transformation. In this section, I will take you through some of the biggest hurdles to digital transformation and how to overcome them.

Addressing Common Obstacles and Pitfalls in Digital Transformation Journeys

While the specific challenges and obstacles each company will face on its digital transformation journey will vary depending on its industry, size, and existing maturity, we have found a number of common themes that emerge in these initiatives:

1. Failure to have clarity of strategy and vision: One of the frequent cases or activities where Digital Transformation initiatives fail is not having a clear strategy and vision. Where do you start? What's most important? It's daunting, even paralyzing…without a clear strategy and vision, it's easy to get caught up in the weeds (your organization's social media obsession or its near dependence on Snapchat filters) and totally lose sight of what's really important.
2. Another frustrating trait identified by the panel was siloed teams and the data therein. When the marketing teams focus on their KPIs, sales or IT is motivated by a different set of goals, then the executive board is after something different and other internal teams or functions are all championing their own purpose, you begin to realize how hard it is for companies to row in the same direction for the benefit of the customer or indeed the agility and scope of the company!

3. Legacy systems and processes: Many companies also have legacy systems, processes and ways of working that run through the organization that are difficult to change. These legacy elements can provide serious barriers to the companies' overturning from older systems to the new technology or the way of working that they are claiming and could also cost an organization huge amounts in terms of time and money.
4. Skills and talent gaps. Another significant digital transformation challenge involves a company's lack of expertise in new technology, typically in areas like data analytics, user experience design, machine learning, etc. Many businesses report a shortage of the talent required to drive the capabilities necessary for digital.
5. Resistance to change: Furthermore, digital transformation often necessitates significant shifts in how individuals work and the cultural components of the business. Overcoming resistance to these shifts, and fostering buy-in and engagement across the organization, are often some of the biggest hurdles in any digital transformation journey.

But overcoming these and other challenges will take a holistic approach to digital transformation that tackles people, processes, and technology in equal measure. It will also need strong leadership, a culture of innovation, clear communication, and the willingness to experiment and learn from both successes and failures.

Overcoming Resistance to Change

Overcoming resistance to change is often one of the most challenging factors in the case of digital transformation. This resistance comes in many forms, everything from not wanting to try new technologies to how things have always been done and cultural inertia. What is important to overcome this resistance is to build a culture around innovation and continuous learning. Where it is okay to try things and fail and it is met with a learning experience versus punishment or blame which is a normal reaction in most corporate cultures to something not going exactly as planned.

This also means investing in training and development programs that help employees build the skills and capabilities they will need to be successful in a digital world. This might include formal training programs in areas like data analytics or user experience design, but it will also require less formal means of helping employees to learn and share knowledge, whether that's through hackathons, 'lunch and learn' sessions or any number of other interventions. A further way of overcoming resistance to change is to involve employees directly in the digital transformation processes that the company is going through. This means seeking out their input and feedback on new technologies and processes and involving them in the design and implementation of those changes. This way, by giving employees a sense of ownership and involvement in the transformation process, businesses can help to build buy-in and engagement at all levels of the company.

Building a Digital-First Culture

Successful digital transformation not only requires overcoming resistance to change but also building a digital-first culture within the business. This means fundamentally rethinking the way in which a company operates and placing digital technologies and capabilities at the heart of everything it does. One key aspect of digital culture is a breakdown of the traditional silos and departmental barriers typically found in companies, and encouraging a level of collaboration and cross-functionality that has never been seen in some of the more traditional industries. This may require the creation of new roles or teams that span different functions, such as a digital transformation office or a customer experience team. In addition to new teams, this may require new tools and platforms that make it easier for teams to work together across different locations or time zones.

A second important aspect of a digital-first culture is a focus on data and analytics. This means not just collecting and storing vast amounts of data (which is true for most organizations) but actually using that data to drive decision-making and continuous improvement. It often requires investment in new tools and platforms for data visualization and insights, and it may require the creation of new roles or teams specifically focused on data analytics.

A third important aspect of a digital-first culture is a focus on customer-centricity and user experience. This means putting the needs and preferences of the customer at the center of all decisions and constantly seeking ways to improve the customer experience across touchpoints and channels. It may involve investment in new research and insights capabilities, or the creation of new roles or teams specifically focused on customer experience and user-centered design.

Upskilling and Reskilling the Workforce

As previously noted, one of the biggest challenges of the digital transformation is the skills gap. Companies will need to invest in training and re-training programs to help employees build or update the skills and expertise needed for a digital age. This can include formal training programs such as data analytics, machine learning, or digital marketing, or it could include more informal learning opportunities such as on-site study, mentorship programs, or job rotations.

Another key in upskilling and reskilling is to create a culture of learning that is continuous in an organization. What this means is to help employees take responsibility for their own learning. Providing the support and resources needed in order to train the employee. An example of this is tuition reimbursement programs or providing sponsored training or certifications. Upskilling and reskilling also include having a focus on diversity and inclusion. As digital technologies reshape work, companies need to have a workforce that represents the diversity of customers and communities they serve. In other words, companies will need to recruit from different places and different experiences and provide a work culture inclusive and accepting to everybody.

Digital transformation is important, but it is not easy. If it were easy, everybody would be doing it. Digital transformation can be the essential core competencies for a company to stay relevant and competitive in the rapidly evolving business landscape. The key is 1) bringing a structured approach to digital transformation, 2) addressing the triad of "people, process, and technology" in that order, and 3) building a culture that values innovation, collaboration, and continuous learning will go a long way toward making the right changes and achieving the optimal level of digital transformation for any organization.

CHAPTER 8: GLOBAL EXPANSION AND LOCALIZATION STRATEGIES

We examined common challenges and obstacles that companies face during their digital transformation journey and strategies for how to overcome them. An essential facet of a company's digital transformation is becoming a global technology (or Martech) and sales (or Salestech) organization. In previous chapters, we have talked about the rise and dependency of Martech and Salestech and the functions and goals of the two, but now we will discuss how technology in these areas can help contribute to a company's efforts to become a global company. One thing we will focus on is how Martech and Salestech can help a company grow in foreign markets as companies are looking to grow and expand in digital, one of the challenges they are going to face is being able to market to customers in foreign countries.

Navigating Cultural, Regulatory, and Technological Differences Across Markets

Navigating the myriad of cultural, regulatory, and technological differences across different markets is one of the biggest challenges in global expansion as what works in one market may not work just as successfully in another. Companies need to be make sure that they can adapt their strategies and approaches if necessary.

For instance, cultural distinctions could make a significant impact on how customers view of a brand and how they interact with brands as well as their expectations of what makes for good communications, customer service, and the desired user experience. In some markets being excessively formal in communications could be off-putting to customers, whilst in other more hierarchical markets it may work.

Likewise, regulatory differences between countries and regions pose challenges for global companies. The regulations on data privacy, for example, differ in Europe and the US, and a company operating in more than one of these regions must comply to all of the regulations. Similarly, the rules and regulations on advertising and consumer protection, among others, differ on countries and regions, requiring the global companies to comply to all of them in order to prevent reputational and legal risks.

Lastly, there are also technological differences that can be a challenge for global expansion, particularly in emerging markets where digital infrastructure may not be as advanced or developed. Companies may have to modify their digital strategies and platforms in order to fit the different internet connectivity, device usage, and digital literacy of customers in those markets. In order to effectively navigate these differences companies must use a localized approach to their marketing and sales strategies. This includes thoroughly researching and analyzing the unique needs, preferences, and behaviors of customers in each market to adjust messaging, content and user experience to the markets.

Adapting Martech and Salestech Solutions for Local Relevance

There are several ways companies can adapt their marketing and sales strategies so that they are relevant in different regions and countries. One of the primary ways this is achieved is by leveraging Martech and Salestech solutions that are specifically designed for global expansion and localization. For example, many marketing automation and CRM platforms now offer multi-language and multi-currency support which make it easy to create, publish, and manage content and campaigns at scale that are relevant to different markets around the world. Additionally, many marketing automation and CRM platforms offer integrated solutions for IP-based personalization or geotargeting which allows companies to deliver highly relevant and personalized user experiences to visitors based on their location or other demographic factors.

Similarly, Salestech solutions have advanced to cater to global sales teams with some solutions offering multi-language support for sales enablement content and training materials as well as integrations with global payment and shipping providers. It is also important to consider local compliance requirements and data localization needs when adapting Martech and Salestech solutions for local relevance. This could involve working with your local legal and compliance teams to ensure data collection, storage and usage practices meet local legal requirements, and potentially investing in additional security measures, such as data encryption and access controls.

Cultural Nuances and Localization Strategies

In addition to tweaking your Martech and Salestech solutions for local relevance, it's also critical that you understand the cultural nuances and differences that can impact the effectiveness of your marketing and sales strategies in different markets. For example, in some countries, building personal relationships and trust are the key to successful sales and business development, while in others, a more transactional and data-driven approach is the best way to win new business. Similarly, in some countries, people may be more open to bold and assertive messaging, while in other markets, a more subtle and nuanced approach is needed.

To maneuver around these cultural differences, companies must commit to leveraging local expertise and partnerships to understand and adapt to the unique cultural context on a market-by-market basis. This may entail hiring local marketing and sales teams, working with local agencies and partners, and regularly conducting local market research and customer feedback surveys. Another effective strategy for navigating cultural differences is prioritizing localization at every level of the customer experience—website and app design, customer service and support, everything. This may include creating localized versions of key assets and content, like product descriptions, user manuals, and marketing collateral, as well as offering local language support through chatbots, email, and phone.

Expediting Emerging Markets' Globalization

Enterprises also need to be flexible around the distinct cultural and regulatory differences of mature markets and at the same time build the capability to quickly globalize emerging markets, particularly in Asian, African and Latin American regions. These markets offer significant growth opportunities for enterprises, but also different challenges and considerations. Many emerging markets may have much less digital infrastructure and literacy, for example, which can affect the suitability of digital sales and marketing strategies.

In order to speed up the global merging markets, it is important for companies to take a strategic and proactive method in relation to constructing their digital capabilities and online existence in particular regions. This may include – Investing in local partnerships and infrastructure e.g. setting up local data centers, and working with local telecoms providers to improve internet connectivity and speed. Adapting Martech and Salestech solutions to account for the unique needs and constraints of these markets – e.g. offering mobile-first experiences and integrating with local payment and logistics providers.

Prioritizing customer education and awareness is another highly recommended strategy for accelerating the globalization of emerging markets. Developing content and resources in the local language, to help educate customers about the value and benefits of the company's products and services is a good example of this. Another example is making investments in community outreach and social impact programs to help build trust and credibility with local audiences.

Increasing ROIs of SMEs and Startups' Marketing/Sales

Martech and Salestech solutions can also play a critical role in helping small and medium-sized enterprises (SMEs) and startups increase their marketing and sales ROI in global markets. In many cases, the challenges faced by small organizations going global are more daunting. They may have limited resources and expertise necessary to navigate the perils of different markets and cultures. Using the right Martech and Salestech solutions however, will help them to level the playing field and compete more effectively with the big players.

For example, many marketing automation and CRM platforms now offer affordable, scalable pricing specifically for small businesses, allowing them to access enterprise-grade features and capabilities without breaking the bank. Similarly, many Salestech solutions offer self-service and low code capabilities that enable smaller teams to quickly and easily build localized sales and marketing campaigns.

Another essential strategy for increasing the ROI of your marketing and sales efforts is to prioritize data-driven decision-making and experimentation. Thanks to tools like A/B testing, customer segmentation, and predictive analytics, this is easier and cheaper than ever before for SMEs and startups. It means these organizations can quickly and easily test and optimize their strategies for different markets and audiences, and make smart decisions about where to invest their limited resources.

Scaling Your Growth Engine Across Borders

A successful global expansion and localization also requires that Netflix build a scalable and adaptable 'growth engine' that can be effectively replicated and applied throughout new markets. It is a holistic and integrated model that encompasses people, processes, and technology to ensure a repeatable practice that can be implemented.

Some key strategies for scaling your growth engine across borders include:

1. Investing in global talent and expertise: Building a diverse and globally-minded team that can bring local knowledge and insights to bear on marketing and sales strategies.
2. Establishing global processes and standards: Developing consistent and repeatable processes for localizing content, campaigns, and experiences across different markets and cultures.
3. Leveraging a centralized technology stack: Implementing a unified and scalable Martech and Salestech stack that can

support the company's efforts across multiple regions and languages.
4. Prioritizing data-driven experimentation and optimization: Continuously testing and refining marketing and sales strategies based on data and insights from different markets and audiences.
5. Building a culture of global collaboration and knowledge-sharing: Fostering a company-wide culture of cross-border collaboration and knowledge-sharing, where teams can learn from each other's successes and failures and share best practices and insights.

By implementing these strategies and utilizing the right Martech and Salestech tools, companies can create a true global growth engine that will support their global expansion and localization initiatives across the world. Chapter 7 will discuss some of the industry trends and what Martech and Sales tools will look like down the road, and how can companies start planning for these changes.

CHAPTER 9: FUTURE TRENDS IN MARTECH AND SALESTECH

In the last chapter, we examined how Martech and Salestech are being used today to help companies with global expansion and localization. But in order to predict that, let's look at some trends about what we think the future for Martech and Salestech will be in the next decades and what to prepare for.

Tech Systems Enabling Martech and Salestech Sustained Growth

The important solutions or analytic systems that keep Martech and Salestech grow are:

1. The biggest factors in the rapid continued growth in the Maretch and Salestech industry are the new technologies that are now available that the enterprise now has access to collect, analyze, and act on to the customer data. This also includes:
2. Customer Data Platforms (CDPs): CDPs are consolidated data with indexes that build the basis for customer-centric marketing. They do for first-party data what DMPs have done for third-party data-buying—consolidate all your data. Its job is to collect all known data about customers from all sources, unify all relevant data into customer profiles, and then make this data available to external systems in such a way that the profiles can be used for any marketing purposes. Most CDPs use third-party cookies, which is not surprising since many CDPs are offshoots of DMPs. However, CDPs are evolving to include use of the 1st party cookies (and mobile device IDs) as well (e.g. for use cases like Web-first data onboarding, mid-funnel retargeting, site optimization, and site personalization).
3. Account-Based Execution: Martech and Salestech vendors have begun to provision for vendors to thereby respond to this realization by assisting in the entire marketing-to-sales

execution process, not for company-to-company sales, ABSD (account-based sales development). That having been said, traditional ABM (account-based marketing) technologies are also evolving to enable account-based marketing and advertising orchestration across different vendors for company to company sale, his or her maintaining vendor against company sale, orchestration that also covers measurement, attribution and... new customer acquisition?

4. Mobile Marketing Automation Platforms: While email marketing has become one of the most saturated and least effective forms of marketing over the last few years, mobile marketing has grown to become the unanticipated, referenced hero of Martech and Salestech. As referenced in more detail at the end of this post, much of this is down to Facebook, which has provided advertisers with an easy and effective way to collect user data via app installs.
5. Omni-Channel Attribution & Modeling: Cross-channel attribution modeling has long been one of the buzzier aspects of Martech and Salestech, however, the rise of Snap, and more importantly, Facebook has brought attribution modeling into the mainstream (see "Nathan Will's" post on Facebook's impact marketing automation budgets). Comparison deactivated Facebook against Vero for Glen Allachie Distillers Ltd, Bottling Worldwide Ltd, and Whisky Magazine Subscription Auto Play Skate Park
6. Marketing Operations Management (MOM) Platforms: Most of this post discusses the trend in which many of the enterprise technologies that marketers will use to actually market and sell their products and services, i.e., the dozens of customer technologies, previously referred to as "marketing technology," are evolving to meet the nuanced requirements of the direct enterprise customer.
7. Artificial Intelligence (AI), Machine Learning, Analytics, Data Science, and the Emerging Real-time Marketing Cloud: Analytics programs have been the first and often the only marketing technology that marketers bought on a standalone basis, and analytics platforms were typically the first customer

technologies that marketers bought when they first began to go direct in the mid-to-late nineties.
8. Digital Asset Management Platforms: Digital asset management platforms manage repositories of strategically important marketing assets such as photos, videos, branding templates, etc. DYI Onsite at our HQ in San Francisco. Our company is very different in this respect from our competitors, but don't ask me why or for how long as our CEO/Head of Marketing will have a much better idea.

Exploring Emerging Technologies (AI, ML, CX platforms, IoT, blockchain, metaverse)

New technologies drive much of the change in the Martech and Salestech landscapes and there is certainly no shortage of new technologies driving change in Martech and Salestech today. Just a few of the emerging and enabling technologies that are affecting the way that companies collect, analyze and act on customer data today include:

1. Artificial Intelligence and Machine Learning: AI and ML are having an impact within a spectrum of Martech and Salestech applications including chatbots, virtual assistants, predictive analytics, and personalization engines. As AI and ML continue to advance, they will facilitate increasingly sophisticated and automated marketing and sales processes that shape-shifts according to a customer's real-time requirements and behavior in the market.
2. Customer Experience Platforms: Customer Experience (CX) platforms provide companies with the ability to manage and optimize the full customer journey end-to-end, from early awareness and acquisition, through to post-purchase support and loyalty. By integrating data and insights from myriad touchpoints and channels, these platforms enable companies to deliver far more personalized and seamless experiences, while driving far higher engagement, conversion and retention.
3. Internet of Things (IoT): Heavily related to Big Data, the IoT is the increasingly growing network of devices and sensors

that generate data about how customers interact with their products in the real world. This is what allows them to deliver insights about customer preferences and behaviors, and help marketers to better plan campaigns and sales teams to better target audience.
4. Blockchain. Blockchain is very new still but has the potential to be a huge deal. Blockchain builds on distributed ledger technology which allows for companies to use immutable, decentralized records. This can help improve trust in business transactions. How? Say you went to a certain restaurant last night and it gave you food poisoning. Even though you paid for your meal with your card, the payment typically takes a few days to go through. The bank has to go through several intermediaries before it finds the credit card network's payment gateway. As a result, getting a refund can frequently be a lengthy process. With blockchain, however, that could potentially change. Because it is a decentralized, completely transparent and unalterable protocol, you can simply view a Google Doc which allows you to see that the money has gone from your bank and is now with the restaurant.
5. Metaverse The growing convergence of virtual and physical worlds: As our lives move increasingly online, a new digital space is developing, combining the 360-degree access of the digital with the 3D space of the physical world. The opportunity for a brand is to create a space in which customers can physically interact with it and the product in a truly immersive way, allowing us to treat the physical and digital worlds as one.

Preparing for the Unknown: Staying Ahead of the Curve

As new technologies continue to emerge at a rapid pace, it can be difficult to know which to prioritize. To stay ahead, companies need to be proactive and strategic in their approach to Martech and Salestech adoption, as well being prepared for how rapidly the market will change.

Some key strategies for preparing for the unknown include:
1. Be continuously monitoring and assessing the landscape: companies need to continuously monitor and assess the landscape in the Martech and Salestech space, and proactively identify and evaluate potential impact and relevance to the business. This may involve attending industry conferences and events, engaging in online forums and communities of like-minded professionals, and meeting with vendors and partners to stay abreast of new and emerging solutions.
2. Experiment with new technologies and approaches: to maintain a competitive edge, companies need to be willing to experiment with new technologies and approaches that may not be fully proven or established. This may involve piloting new solutions on a small scale or creating dedicated innovation teams that are responsible for exploring and testing new concepts and ideas.
3. Building a culture of innovation and agility: To truly future-proof their businesses, marketers must foster a culture of innovation and agility that encourages experimentation, risk-taking, and continuous learning. They will need to build new organizational structures and processes that allow for faster decision-making and execution and invest more in training and development programs that help employees build new skills and capabilities.
4. Collaborating with partners and ecosystems: Given the complexity and fast pace of change in the Martech and Salestech landscape, marketers cannot go it alone. To stay ahead of the curve, marketers must actively collaborate with partners and ecosystems that can provide them with access to new technologies, expertise, and resources. This might involve joining industry consortia or alliances, working with start-ups or academic institutions, or participating in open-source communities and projects.

Predictions for the Evolution of Martech and Salestech

These are not facts, they are predictions. No one has a crystal ball but there are things that we are starting to see emerge trends, and that will emerge over the coming years:

1. The gap between the Martech and Salestech will blur even more in 2020. The Martech and Salestech solutions will definitely cover even more. More and more people are looking for "super platforms" that will be "the-only-place-I-need-to-go" solutions across the entire customer lifecycle (marketing and sales) so there will certainly be a convergence here. This will also lead to an increase in M&A activity as the larger vendors will look to add new capabilities and technologies to their offerings.
2. There is an increased focus on security and privacy. More and more people do not trust using customer data for them to better sell to those customers. Vendors will start to put privacy and security as part of their solution, period. GDPR and CCPA will become more widely adopted and more and more people will look for secure multi-party computation, encryption, and blockchain solutions to ensure no misuse of customer data.
3. Automation and personalization aided by AI: As machine learning and AI technologies become more advanced, we can expect to see even higher levels of automation and personalization throughout the marketing and sales process. The not-too-distant future will likely mean AI chatbots and virtual assistants fielding routine customer interactions and inquiries, while predictive analytics and recommendation engines better serve prospective customers in real-time with exactly what they need.
4. Additionally, Customer data platforms (CDP) are another marketing technology that will affect digital marketing next year. The likes of customer data platforms will be driven to popularity, and have a big effect on the digital marketing technology landscape in 2020/21, as customer journeys now demand that marketing understands the customer on an end-to-end basis, as they transact and interact across disparate touchpoints and channels. A CDP is marketing software that aggregates, analyses and gives access to a business of unified,

cleansed, deduplicated customer data and its antecedents, and uses that data to enable marketing, from a single platform, that delivers the audience-optimized, personalized and consistent user experiences that, in turn, drive more efficient and effective marketing and sales. This will then give a more reliable and accurate target audience.
5. Similarly, as the landscape continues to change dramatically over the next few years, countless new business models and revenue streams will emerge that "tech-enable" the business function. For instance, some companies may begin charging a subscription for customers to access the data and insights that are produced from their different algorithms. Alternatively, companies may invent new types of products and services that are completely underwritten and powered by AI and ML algorithms that create entirely new markets and methods of growing and differentiating their company and quite possibly, entirely new paradigms around how value is created and captured in the digital age.

New Frontiers in Marketing and Sales Technology

Looking beyond the immediate horizon, there are several new frontiers in marketing and sales technology that are likely to emerge in the coming years. We predict the following:

1. Expect to see a surge in Augmented and Virtual Reality technologies as most of the various systems graduate out of development. You will see far greater adoption of these technologies in marketing and sales scenarios. Companies may begin to include AR features such as product demonstrations or visualizations in mobile apps or experiences you can use. Companies may begin to include VR features such as virtual events or customer environments in mobile apps or experiences you can use.
2. Voice and conversational interfaces: More companies are building voice and conversational interfaces as customers start to become familiar with these interfaces and the devices such

as Amazon's Alexa and Google's Google Assistant. This means that a company builds custom skills or applications to allow customers to access products and services by natural language commands and queries alone.
3. Neuro Marketing and Bio Data: As our understanding of the human brain and body continues to advance, so does our ability to look at new ways to use that to manipulate consumers. I expect we'll see more and more marketers looking to neuromarketing and bio data to help inform their thinking on how to communicate and target customers. Things like eye tracking, facial recognition, and even EEG technology to measure the brain's response to marketing stimuli in real time will inform adjustments to marketing campaigns and messaging. Stay tuned on this one for sure.
4. Quantum Computing and Advanced Analytics: While it is still in fairly early stages, there is a lot of excitement about the prospects and potential impact of quantum computing on our ability to process — and mine — huge amounts of customer data. Essentially, quantum computing processes data at different levels and can therefore offer insights that are impossible via traditional computing when it comes to things like complex simulation and optimization. Think of it as a whole new level of insight for marketers that can enable a greater degree of personalization and targeting and produce a far more accurate set of predictive models and forecasts.

The future of Martech and Salestech in a sense will be all about a business with more and faster change and innovations. In this business successful marketing and sales organizations will be those who can quickly react and make proactive, strategic, and agile decisions around trends as they emerge; whether it's new technologies like AI, ML, and CX platforms or more advanced another sophisticated versions of everything else. If you involve these technologies in your company you will win in the Martech and Salestech space.

What the future holds for marketing and sales is the story of companies that will be the first to make technology work for them, creating value both for their customers and for their stakeholders. The companies who will beat market projections and be the biggest winners in Marketing new frontier are those who will push these technologies to the limit and stay on the far prospects of the bell curve, creating untold competitive advantage and growth opportunities for many years to come.

CHAPTER 10: SUCCESS CASES FOR REFERENCES

In this chapter, you will find nine very interesting case studies that presented how leading companies belonging to various industries have leveraged Martech and Salestech solutions to achieve amazing results in the age of the digital! These cases are proof of how Martech and Salestech are neither a bubble nor a trend, it is the testimony of the incredible transformations they have brought or are bringing to companies and they provide tips to improve your marketing and sales strategies right now.

1. Coca-Cola's "Share a Coke" Campaign:

Coca-Cola is a worldwide company producing carbonated beverages. Artificial Intelligence was used to scan social media to determine the most popular names and trendy sayings with customers. Then they put those names and sayings on their Coca-Cola bottles and get their customers to take pictures and post them to social media just by using the hashtag #ShareaCoke. This created a nationwide wildfire movement bringing tons of brand awareness and sales with it. Coca-Cola says tens of thousands of bottles were shared in the success of the "Coca-Cola Summer Love campaign", working in partnership with Macys, which saw sales rise 19% along with a 7% increase in young adult consumption. Drinking Coke is very personable to people and Coca-Cola realized that, How? By using artificial intelligence on which names were most popular on sites such as Facebook and Twitter. The use of geotargeting further enhanced the campaign by include local names for local people.

The "Share a Coke" campaign was a major success and social media played a role in that. There were over 500,000 photos shared on social media, a 2% increase in soft-diet sales reversing a decade-long downward trend in sales since 1997, a 12% increase in followers on social media, and a 7% increase in positive sentiment about the Coke brand. By using AI and personalization Coca-Cola created an emotional connection, generated buzz, and ultimately drove business.

2. Sephora's Personalized Beauty Experience:

Leading beauty retailer, Sephora revolutionized the customer experience by leveraging Martech solutions in their mobile app. Using AI and machine learning algorithms, Sephora's mobile app used to Martech to deliver personalized product recommendations based on customer's skin types, preferences, and purchase history. The mobile app also leverages AR-based virtual try-on tools and a loyalty program to increase engagement and value. Sephora's Martech has resulted in a significant increase in mobile orders and sales overall, by creating a seamless beauty experience.

Sephora's Personalized web experience was so successful that the retailer saw a 75% increase in mobile order revenue and a 20% lift in overall sales. Their try-and-buy feature was also met with very high engagement, with shoppers spending an average of 10 minutes per session trying on different makeup looks, and a loyalty program integration with the mobile app saw members spending 2.5 times more than non-members, aimed at boosting customer retention. This is a perfect example of how a company can successfully put Martech at the heart of their business to create a truly customer-centric experience that brings true value to both the customer and the business.

3. Marketo's Marketing Automation Success:

Marketo, a popular marketing automation platform, is proof that its technology works. They used their own solution to overhaul the way they generated and nurtured leads and used Martech optimally to deploy AI-powered lead scoring, a full-featured email campaign platform that supported personalization at scale, a data warehouse and BI platform connected to their CRM, and Account-based marketing. Part of their process included implementing an efficient onboarding process for new clients (called their 'Secret Sauce') designed to get them into market-up and driving ROI as quickly as possible. Result: Marketo almost doubled the size their sales pipeline and fast-tracked their way to much faster revenue growth.

The use of its own platform, helped Marketo see a 60% increase in its sales pipeline and a 25% increase in revenue. Marketo's AI-powered lead scoring system helped them to determine which leads were most valuable, resulting in a 30% increase in conversions from leads to opportunities. They also saw a 50% increase in open rates and a 25% increase in clickthrough rates with personalized emails versus generic emails. Not only did their personalized emails perform better than the generic emails, but their account-based marketing strategies also outperformed, with target accounts seeing a 40% increase in engagement and a 20% increase in deal size.

4. Cisco's Salestech-Powered Sales Enablement:

During Dreamforce, Cisco showcased the power of Salestech in relation to its world-class networking technology. Cisco was able to integrate its CRM system with a marketing automation platform. This allowed their Salesforce to enable sales reps to have a unified view of the interactions and preferences of their customers. AI-powered algorithms analyzed the data to bring real-time insights and recommendations to the sales reps. By using AI-powered chatbots, Cisco was able to further the enhancement of support to their customers while allowing the sales reps to focus on the higher value interactions. The deployment of these Salestech solutions for Cisco resulted in a significant increase in their sales productivity and sales revenue

The software was a success story. It achieved 30% better conversion rates on the leads generated using time-tracking software and full process automation. It also recorded a 20% uplift in hunting deals and a 15% uplift in average deal size. The artificial intelligence features built into the software helped sellers identify up-spend and cross-sell opportunities, achieving a 20% uplift in revenue per customer. Cisco further increased customer satisfaction by turning to customer service chatbots. Satisfaction increased by 60%, even as costs fell by 70%.

5. Airbnb's Personalized Travel Marketplace:

A Marketplace For Hosting And Discovering Holiday Rentals Officially launched in August 2008, Airbnb is a trusted online marketplace for people to list, discover, and book unique holiday rentals around the world. Airbnb uses machine learning and AI to analyze data across its busy marketplace to create a personalized experience for each of its users. By offering search results and recommendations tailored to the specific history, preferences, and needs of individual users, Airbnb significantly increases its booking rates and referral revenue. Furthermore, its dynamic pricing algorithms benefit hosts by advising them on how to maximize their listing prices in periods of high demand or seasonality, therefore providing them with a 10% uplift in revenues. Airbnb's success emphasizes the power of using AI and machine learning to create a more targeted, efficient marketplace.

6. Starbucks' Loyalty Program and Personalization:

Starbucks, a worldwide coffee chain, used Martech to improve their customer experience with their mobile app and loyalty rewards program. By utilizing the app's AI powered recommendations, mobile ordering and loyalty rewards program Starbucks was able to create a high level of customer convenience, loyalty, and spending. By using Martech to create an easy and rewarding experience, Starbucks saw mobile transactions making up 30% of total sales as well as a significant increase in customer loyalty and revenue.

Starbucks' mobile app and loyalty program have seen a 25% increase in customer visit frequency and a 40% increase in average spend per visit. Customized product recommendations are seeing conversion rates 50% higher than non-personalized, while 20% of all transactions are now mobile orders. Starbucks' loyalty program now has 15% more members year on year, with a total of 50% of all transactions coming from members. This serves as a great example of what Martech can do in terms of driving customer engagement and loyalty.

7. HubSpot's Inbound Marketing and Sales Alignment:

Creating SEO-optimized, gated content to attract leads, sending captivating, personalized automated emails to nurture them through to becoming MQLs, using AI for lead scoring to accurately determine when a lead was worthy of being handed over to Sales, and utilizing the integration between their CRM and MAP platforms to ensure a smooth hand-off and experience between departments. As a result of being able to pour their own Kool-Aid, HubSpot was able to: Increase website traffic by 50% — giving a bump in telemarketing names; and Drive a 40% increase in revenue.

Instead of spending enormous amounts of money on marketing, advertisements, and emails with no success; HubSpot decided to take a different route. HubSpot decided to take an inbound approach that allows the customer to reach out to HubSpot only if they're interested in what the company has to offer. HubSpot relied on personal nurturing emails other than general e-mails being sent to customers as well as AI-powered leads scoring to only reach out to the leads with promising results. Through these tactics, HubSpot was able increase the lead generation by three times after using the inbound tactic. The average number of sales made after using the marketing tactic went up by 20 percent. Since HubSpot believed in rapid response time between the customer and the buyer, it allowed the company to score the highest in customer satisfaction.

8. Nike's Personalized Shopping Experience:

This global, sporting brand, used Martech to create a personal, omnichannel shopping experience. They achieved this through Martech by using AI to give product recommendations, creating targeted promotions and displays in-store while using this technology to track every interaction to further develop a customer profile. As a result, online sales rose by 30% and customer loyalty and repeat purchases increased.

There is a suggestion that over 70% of Nike's users interacted with AI-powered fashion bots on the site, lifting conversion rates by 40%. Meanwhile, geotargeted promotions increased redemption by 25%, increasing both sales and foot traffic. Additionally, interactive in-store displays drove a 20% increase in "time spent and product engagement" and helped customers make "more informed buying decisions."

More pointedly, those customers who engaged with Nike via personalized recommendations opted to spend 23% more. Geo-targeted promotions led to a 30% increase in spending in-store and interactive displays resulted in customers spending 20% longer in store. The result was also a 15% increase in customer lifetime value with users returning at a 20% clip.

9. Salesforce's AI-Powered Sales Forecasting and Coaching:

Salesforce is a leading global provider of CRM and Sales technology that employs Artificial Intelligence to effectively boost sales forecasting and coaching. Using the Salesforce Einstein AI platform, Salesforce analyzed huge amounts of sales data, which helped to improve sales forecasting allowing sales representatives to enjoy up-to-the-minute accurate forecasts and insights. This in turn allowed them to have the insights to enable them to better prioritize their time and effort on closing opportunities. Moreover, Salesforce used its new platform called MyTrailhead to offer personalized coaching and learning based on individual skill and performance. With the aid of Salesforce AI and MyTrailhead, Salesforce reported a huge increase in sales productivity of 25% and a 20% increase in revenue.

Salesforce's Einstein AI platform has delivered impressive results — by using AI to provide sales reps with a more complete view of their customers, the company increased sales forecast accuracy by 30%, resulting in more informed business decisions while ensuring that the sales organization has the necessary resources to close deals. Plus, the AI platform identified at-risk deals and delivered critical recommendations to sales reps, helping them course-correct and achieve a 15% improvement in win rates. Recognizing the value of personalized coaching, the company introduced MyTrailhead to better develop sales professionals. Now, reps are 20% more productive and new hires achieve full productivity (ramp-up) at a 25% faster rate. MyTrailhead has also contributed to a 15% uptick in sales quota attainment companywide. Given these results, it's evident that AI has the power to significantly boost sales performance and business growth.

Success stories of well-known international companies from a range of industries help to illustrate just how much potential Martech and Salestech can offer in terms of business growth and enhanced customer experiences. By creating a strategy and adopting these two technologies in a smart way, backed by a solid knowledge of personalization, automation, AI-powered insights, and seamless cross-channel experiences, you will distinguish your business from competitors, bring people closer to your brand, and achieve impressive results in the digital era.

The ever-evolving landscape of marketing and sales demands that companies constantly keep current on advances in Martech and Salestech and re-evaluating which of these solutions can be integrated into the company's overall strategy. By taking cues from the successes of industry leaders in the field, and making them fit their needs and their goals specifically, companies can best utilize transformative technologies to gain a competitive edge in an increasingly digital marketplace.

ACKNOWLEDGEMENT

In the creation of this seminal series, I have had the distinct privilege of drawing upon the invaluable experiences, insights, and expertise generously shared by a distinguished global network of esteemed partners and accomplished friends. Their direct and indirect contributions have been instrumental, and it is with profound gratitude that I acknowledge the indelible influence they have had on this work.

<u>Kanth Krishnan</u>: Managing Director at Accenture, has been a beacon of inspiration with his incisive insights and visionary leadership in technology services. His profound depth of knowledge and innovative approach have significantly enriched the content of this book.

As Managing Director at Newmark, <u>Jeff Pappas</u> has provided critical perspectives on the dynamic global real estate market landscape. His unparalleled expertise has contributed to a deeper understanding of the business environments explored herein.

<u>Haitao Qi</u>, Chairman of Devott Research and Advisory, has provided exceptionally enlightening perspectives on technology innovations and market trends, especially in the Asian context.

Formerly leading Outsourcing and Managed Services at PwC, <u>Charles Aird</u>'s comprehensive knowledge and strategic foresight in outsourcing services have greatly contributed to my understanding of this critical business function.

It has been my great privilege to learn from and collaborate with these distinguished individuals and institutions operating at the leading edge of our industry. Any merits of this book stem directly from the exceptional global network of friends and partners upon whom I rely. Any faults or shortcomings are solely my own.

Last but not least, the unwavering understanding and support of my beloved wife, Biyu, has been an inspiration to this professional endeavor. The intensive writing workload harkened back to my doctoral dissertation at Yale a quarter-century ago. She remains the driving force behind my career growth and personal fulfillment.

ABOUT THE AUTHOR

Stephan S. Sunn

Stephan Sunn is the Executive Partner at Sanford Black Advisory, a preeminent global business and investment consultancy. In this capacity, he collaborates with industry leaders to advise companies worldwide on growth strategy, marketing/sales, innovation monetization, partnerships, and mergers & acquisitions. Over the past two decades, Mr. Sunn has consulted on sourcing provider selection for more than 30 international corporations and over 20 investment and M&A deals in the technology services, digital technologies, and global outsourcing sectors.

Mr. Sunn possesses particular expertise in empowering private enterprises to accelerate growth and enhance value creation through engagement with governments and technology parks. He holds a leadership position with Devott Co., China's largest private research firm focused on the IT, software, and technology services industries. Additionally, he serves as a Director at the China IT and Outsourcing Association. His clients span Fortune 500 companies, state-owned enterprises, technology parks, SMBs, and startups in both developed and emerging markets.

A graduate of the University of Science and Technology of China (USTC) with a Bachelor of Science degree, and Yale University with a Master of Science and Ph.D., Mr. Sunn frequently shares his insights and research as a speaker at global conferences and events. He is a prolific author and an accomplished presenter for his projects and clients around the world.

BOOKS BY THIS AUTHOR

Competing For The Growth

This book serves as a guidebook for city planners, economic development professionals, tech park builders, and public officials who aim to create thriving innovation communities that attract global trade and stimulate investments. It offers a structured path that begins with intangible factors like vision setting and partnership alignment and extends to pilots and full-blown magnet programs. The book provides real-life instructions to help put these ideas into practice, including effective strategies for attracting rapidly growing businesses and talent, creating a setting that promotes innovation and entrepreneurship, fostering a competitive and appealing business climate, and building a globally recognized brand and reputation. The author emphasizes that cities and tech parks must play to their strengths and assets to compete and win in the global arena. The race for relevance is on, and the window of opportunity to determine the outcome is closing. Cities and companies have what they need to succeed, and with the options, relationships, and guidance provided in this book, city managers and tech park authorities can make the decisions necessary to lead their communities to success in the world investment and trade arena.

Searching the New Profits

In the face of global market turbulence and domestic uncertainties, American small and medium-sized businesses (SMBs) and startups have significant growth opportunities in emerging markets. However, these markets also present unique challenges. This handbook provides a semi-analytical and semi-prescriptive approach to help American SMBs and entrepreneurs succeed in these rapidly expanding markets. Conversely, governments, technology parks, and corporations in emerging countries can utilize this book to learn how to collaborate with U.S. companies in their markets to serve their customers effectively.

The book covers essential themes such as researching and identifying matching markets, choosing the appropriate market entry mode, local marketing and sales tactics, effective risk management, establishing an active and reputable presence in the local market, ensuring full legal compliance, avoiding political involvement, talent search and retention, and balancing standardization and localization. The final chapter shares valuable lessons from decades of business practices, acknowledging that readers may have different perspectives on these topics. Expanding knowledge through diverse viewpoints is beneficial for U.S. SMB and startup leaders. Despite the challenges, penetrating foreign markets can be highly profitable, and U.S. enterprises have a reasonable chance of success by capitalizing on the vast potential of these rapidly growing territories.

Cracking the Winning Codes

This book serves as a comprehensive guide for international technology and outsourcing companies seeking to enter and succeed in the highly competitive U.S. market. It emphasizes the importance of adapting to the unique American business culture, which values innovation, diversity, relationships, customer-centricity, and results-oriented management. The guide highlights the need to navigate the complex U.S. regulatory landscape, including federal and state laws, as well as key legislations such as FCPA, SOX, and HIPAA.

The book covers essential topics such as understanding American business culture, complying with legal requirements, developing effective marketing strategies, employing successful sales techniques, addressing cultural differences, and managing risks associated with entering a new market. Additionally, it encourages the use of innovative tactics to differentiate from competitors and gain market share.

A special section titled "The Lessons" shares the author's personal experiences and insights, providing practical execution tips that focus on solution-oriented approaches, leveraging referrals and testimonials, managing communication costs, delivering higher quality than promised, and investing in proven local sales leaders.

By adhering to the core principles of understanding buyer preferences, continuous innovation, human capital development, risk management, customer-centricity, and resilient operations, global providers can successfully navigate and thrive in the lucrative U.S. market.

Renovations or Revolutions

The book "Renovation or Revolution? Impacts of Latest AI on BPO and Contact-centers Industries" provides an in-depth exploration of the transformative potential of artificial intelligence (AI) within the business process outsourcing (BPO) and contact center industries. It emphasizes the importance of early adoption, customization, and localization of AI solutions to gain a competitive edge in the global marketplace. The book highlights the evolving role of human agents, who will focus on complex problem-solving and relationship-building, while AI handles routine tasks. It also discusses the development of AI expertise within organizations and the ethical considerations surrounding AI implementation.

The authors present a roadmap for incorporating AI, underlining the need for a clear vision, employee training, and continuous improvement. Looking ahead, the book envisions a future of collaborative human-AI partnerships, hyper-personalization, and proactive customer engagement. It stresses that embracing AI is crucial for BPO and contact center companies to achieve sustainable growth and remain competitive in the international arena. The book serves as a comprehensive guide for executives navigating the AI revolution in the global business services industry.

Risky Reefs in the Ocean of Global Markets

This book provides a comprehensive roadmap for emerging market companies venturing into global expansion. It highlights common pitfalls across strategic planning, finance, operations, human resources, marketing, technology, legal/ethics, and risk management. The book emphasizes thorough market research, cultural adaptation,

local partnerships, brand building, innovation investment, and long-term vision.
As the global landscape evolves, it anticipates trends like digitization, sustainability integration, and talent acquisition challenges. The book provides corporate decision-makers with insights and best practices to navigate complexities, mitigate risks, and foster sustainable growth while driving innovation and progress internationally.

The AI revolution in B2B Marketing and Sales

This professional guidance provides a comprehensive playbook for leveraging artificial intelligence (AI) to drive measurable results in B2B marketing and sales strategies. With insights from real-world case studies spanning diverse industries and business sizes, it explores AI's transformative impact on understanding the AI-empowered buyer, delivering personalized omnichannel experiences, boosting sales productivity, and optimizing operations.
The book offers a strategic framework for successful AI implementation, covering data readiness, talent acquisition, governance, and ethical considerations. Globally applicable principles foster human-AI collaboration, enabling organizations worldwide to harness AI's potential ethically and profitably in the B2B domain.

Promotor, Suppressor or Neutralizer

This book explores how artificial intelligence (AI) and geopolitics are
transforming the global outsourcing industry. It analyzes the strategic
implications of AI for outsourcing operations, delivery models, talent
management, and client relationships. The impact of geopolitical forces like
trade tensions, political instability, and regulatory shifts on risk mitigation
and geographic diversification is examined.

Emerging business models combining AI and human expertise, niche
services, innovation through collaboration, workforce upskilling, and ethical AI governance are highlighted. The book provides a strategic roadmap for international outsourcing providers to navigate challenges,
seize opportunities, and drive sustainable growth in this era of technological
disruption and evolving geopolitical dynamics.

Pricing for Profitability and Growth

This book explores how companies in the technology and service sectors can leverage strategic pricing to drive growth and profitability. It advocates moving beyond traditional cost-plus pricing to adopt value-based approaches that align pricing with customer perceptions of value. Key recommendations include: conducting thorough market research to understand customer needs and willingness to pay; segmenting customers and offering differentiated pricing tiers; leveraging data and analytics for dynamic pricing optimization; and aligning sales, marketing and pricing teams around a cohesive value proposition. The book emphasizes the importance of quantifying and communicating value to justify premium pricing.

Looking to the future, the book highlights how artificial intelligence and machine learning will transform pricing capabilities, enabling more personalized and responsive pricing strategies. It cautions against common pitfalls like failing to account for competitive responses or neglecting the psychology of pricing. Ultimately, the authors argue that pricing is a critical strategic capability that requires ongoing experimentation, cross-functional collaboration, and a willingness to adapt to changing market conditions. By taking a customer-centric, data-driven approach to pricing, technology and service companies can gain a powerful lever for sustainable growth and competitive advantage.

www.ingramcontent.com/pod-product-compliance
Lightning Source LLC
Chambersburg PA
CBHW050235230526
45470CB00005B/1965